What others are saying about

The Next Level Navigator®

George Black has created steps necessary for soul searching and implementing to become a successful entrepreneur.
~ Garrett Takach, competitor on NBC's American Ninja Warrior and founder of Ninja Park

The Next Level Navigator is strategy without all the BS!
~ Shaun Lee, founder of Truckin' Tomato

George and Intigro have a process [The Next Level Navigator] *that brings order to disarray and can help any organization focus its efforts on the key drivers of success.*
~ Lew Moorman, former President of Rackspace

We had the good fortune of bumping into George at just the right time as we built Rackspace from an idea into a global company. George's ideas and passion helped us really elevate our ability to build a great company. I'm grateful for the contribution George made to us and recommend his work to anyone aspiring to build a great company.
~ Lanham Napier, former CEO of Rackspace

For Rackspace, Intigro [George Black] *helped the leaders of a critical new business unit create its strategy for success, and helped roll out key financial metrics. After that success, George led all our corporate off-site meetings for many years using his Next Level Navigator process. From 2004-2008, George coached many members of our leadership team to keep our strategy on track while we grew more than 50% per year. George delivered great results. I recommend him and Intigro to any business.*
~ Graham Weston, former Chairman of Rackspace

[George Black] *provides great step-by-step processes used to execute/implement any entrepreneurial endeavor that anyone has a passion for.* [He] *shows one how to deal with disruptions, develop strategies, and think outside the box.*
~ Keith Ditta, entrepreneur

THE [ONE HOUR] NEXT LEVEL NAVIGATOR

George Black

intigrō Press

Copyright © 2018 by George Black
Published by Intigro Press, LLC and in association with Intigro, Inc.

All worldwide rights reserved. No portion of this book may be reproduced, stored in a retrieval system, or transmitted in any form or by any means - electronic, mechanical, photocopy, recording, scanning, or other - except for brief quotations in critical reviews or articles, without the prior written permission of the author.

Limit of Liability/Disclaimer of Warranty: While the Author, the Publisher, and Intigro, Inc. have used their best efforts in preparing this book, they make no representations or warranties with respect to the accuracy or completeness of the contents of this book and specifically disclaim any implied warranties of merchantability or fitness for a particular purpose. No warranty may be created or extended by sales representatives or any sales materials, written, video or otherwise. The advice and strategies contained herein may not be suitable for your situation. You should consult with a professional where appropriate. Neither the Author, the Publisher, or Intigro, Inc. shall be liable for any loss of profit or any other commercial damages, including but not limited to special, incidental, consequential, or other damages which is incurred as a consequence, directly or indirectly, of the use and application of any of the contents of this work.

The names and identifying characteristics of any individuals portrayed in the book are purely fictional, any resemblance to individuals living or dead is coincidental.

The Intigro logo and name and the term "Success Barriers" are trademarks of Intigro, Inc. and used with permission. The term "The Next Level Navigator" is a registered trademark of Intigro, Inc. and used with permission. The logo and name "Live Truly Free" is a trademark of Live Truly Free, LLC and used with permission.

All quotes noted are from *The Next Level Entrepreneur: Focus your Passions · Map your Direction · Build a Great Company.* [*The NLE*] Copyright © 2013, 2015, 2018 by George Black. Used by permission of Intigro Press, LLC and in association with Intigro, Inc. All worldwide rights reserved.

For bulk orders and pricing please contact orders@intigropress.com.

ISBN-13: 978-0-9995746-1-4

For more resources please visit
www.LiveTrulyFree.com

For those men and women with a vision for anything.

The [One Hour] Next Level Navigator is yours to achieve;
should you fail, a mediocre life is yours to receive.
Complete this challenge and you will see,
the truer person you are intended to be.
— George Black

"The [person] who has lost the spirit of youth is too busy with gloomy forecasts...*

[People] with the spirit of youth pioneered our America...

[People] with vision and sturdy confidence. They found contentment in the thrill of action, knowing that

success was never final and failure never fatal.
It was courage that counted.

Isn't opportunity in America today greater than it was in the days of our grateful forefathers?"

Live Life... Every golden minute of it

~ excerpted from a 1938 Anheuser-Busch Ad

---

* The words 'person' and 'people' have been substituted for the original words 'man' and 'men' to reflect the quote's intent in today's parlance.

~ Contents ~

Preface: Why [One Hour]?..................................viii
Greetings!..1
    How to best use this little book...........................3
    The Map..4
    Tips for applying The Navigator to various
    circumstances 6
    Establish a High Camp 7
The [One Hour] process starts here, so...
Let's Begin your Assault 11
    Dreams to Envisioning...12
    Your Next Level..16
    Success Barriers..22
    Next Strategic Steps...24
    The [One Hour] Next Level Navigator instructions
    (page 26) & final form (page 27)..........................26
    One Hour +, if you have 5 minutes 28
A Closing Word from George 30
More resources to reach your Next Level!...............31
    About the Author 32
Your Personal Notes & Insights 33

How to Maximize this book!

1. Read the entire book (including all the prompts), which could take about 30 to 45 minutes.
2. If you haven't read all of *The NLE*, then read all the pages sourced from it, referenced throughout this book.
3. Establish a High Camp & follow the guidance on page 8.
4. **Start your timer for the [One Hour] on page 11!**

Preface: Why [One Hour]?

We live in an age of 'click this' or 'swipe that' and it instantly appears. If the spinning wheel pops up, we often don't wait and will bounce to something else. Right?

Establishing Next Levels are not a click away or a swipe. They take time to discover.

Whenever I have guided a company's leadership team through The Next Level Navigator® process, I typically allow a couple of days with the team away from their business. They need time to decompress, focus, discover and create. I handle the prep before the offsite and afterwards translate their ideas and strategies into The Next Level Navigator their company will use.

Ultimately this is a great value for them, because it is time efficient for the executives and they benefit from all my experience of doing Navigators. The cost to the company for this service pales in relation to the returns they will achieve over the next 3 to 5 years by reaching their Next Level.

So what is the downside to this approach? Only a handful of companies a year can benefit from my help and they rarely internalize the process.

My Passion

I love entrepreneurs! I know them well, for I am one too! In fact, this is *the reason* I wrote *The Next Level Entrepreneur: Focus your Passions · Map your Direction · Build a Great Company*, [*The NLE*] available on Amazon.com. For I desire everyone to experience The Next Level Navigator.

I, also, know that if a person likes an idea, they are ready to start immediately, especially entrepreneurs! We don't want to wait for availability, or spend days doing it, not to mention the cost.

Preface

So, what do we do instead?

Frankly, many of us 'shoot first', then we might steady ourselves, and aiming is probably an afterthought. The letter "Ready, Fire, Aim" has a more complete consideration of this observation. [page 117-119, *The NLE (Next Level Entrepreneur)*]

The [One Hour] Next Level Navigator is designed specifically for those who are ready to start right now! I wrote this book so you could "get ready, AIM, then fire" very quickly! How about that!?!

But, Next Levels still need to be discovered.

Creating Great Art!

Strategizing, crafting and writing a great Next Level Navigator is similar to creating a great piece of art.

For example, to fashion a fabulous bronze sculpture takes considerable time, even for a great artist who has years of experience. The sculptor will begin by making a small, clay model of the final work. In fact, they often make numerous models before they are satisfied. It is only then that they will make the final sculpture to the scale they intend.

This book, *The [One Hour] Next Level Navigator*, is the equivalent of making a clay model before doing the final sculpture.

Allow me to be honest with you, your first Navigator will not be very good for 2 reasons:

- Like the sculptor, the first one is never very good when compared to the final one.
- Unlike the sculptor, you probably have little to no experience doing Navigators.

But do not be discouraged. Instead, recognize the rarity of your intentions with this process, as so few entrepreneurs truly 'aim' before they 'fire'.

Preface

In fact, be encouraged! For when you have done it once, it is easier to do again and again. I have seen that the more times a person or a team does The Next Level Navigator, the better their Navigators become.

Creating great art requires stamina, persistence, and practice, much like scaling a great mountain peak! This strategic process requires a similar diligence. And, I have every confidence that you will succeed!

The Navigator in only One Hour

But, read *The NLE* [*Next Level Entrepreneur*]**, first!**

The [One Hour] Next Level Navigator is condensed from the complete Navigator process contained in Part 3 of *The Next Level Entrepreneur.* [*The NLE*]

Your best results will occur if you have read the entire book, especially Part 3. But if you are anxious to get started, read all the *The NLE* pages sourced.

The idea behind this shorter version is to help the user finish their Navigator as fast as possible for all the aforementioned reasons. But there is something else.

Early on, I thought it was better to labor in creating a great first Navigator. But inevitably, I discovered that the second one I did was always better. And that is when I shifted.

Now, I believe it is better to do them fast, often, and *not* perfect. In fact, plan on doing another one in a few months.

Space does not permit me to elaborate as to all the why's and wherefore's, so I will jump to my conclusion. After all these years of doing Navigators I have come to fervently believe:

Any Strategy is better than No Strategy, and...

Any Next Level is better than No Next Level!

Whether you are seeking The Next Level for your personal self or career or startup business endeavor or ongoing company, my hope is to propel you to live more and more into the person you are intended to be. And as you draw on the truest parts of you, my dream is for you to ultimately live truly free.

More Resources on the Way

Once you complete this little book, I have an idea that you will want more! Such as doing The [Complete] Next Level Navigator, more "Sage Advice Applications" as found in *The NLE*, more ideas and more help that we may offer.

To that end, this book is the first of more resources and books to accompany *The NLE*. We are planning to offer numerous online helps at www.LiveTrulyFree.com, interactive online events, and perhaps even live seminars.

We would love to hear from you! What would really help you? We welcome you ideas, input, and what you might be needing at IdeasFor@livetrulyfree.com!

Also, we are looking for people who would be interested in becoming Certified Next Level Navigator Guides to lead others in this process. Maybe that could be you!?!

So, please sign up for our newsletter to keep up with all the new resources, as they become available at:

www.LiveTrulyFree.com

Now, it's time to begin.

But, I must warn you...

Turn this page, only if you truly want to play. Because, you will find yourself sucked in and doing *The [One Hour] Next Level Navigator* before you realize what is happening.

For now, I will be your guide.

So if you dare, go ahead... turn the page.

~ George Black, July 2018

Greetings!

Brave reader and gamer, welcome to *The [One Hour] Next Level Navigator*! I have been quite anxious awaiting your arrival.

I am George Black, the author of *The Next Level Entrepreneur*. And, I will be your guide.

As you may or may not know, you are in serious danger of living a mediocre life. My objective is to help you find yours or your company's Next Level. And, launch you into your first step towards it. You will have exactly One Hour to complete this mission.

Should you fail you will lose a 'life'. If you lose 3 'lives', it is game over and you must live the rest of your actual life at the level you are at today! Just kidding!

Or, am I?

You see most people rarely dare to risk. They just seem to settle wherever life drops them off. Oh, occasionally they may see something that appears better and head off in that direction. And for a while, they may feel upbeat and even encouraged. But eventually, they tire and life settles back into routine, as usual.

"Why is that?", you may ask.

Mr. A explains it this way to Max: *"Any one with a vision for anything is an entrepreneur. However, life becomes a real adventure for those who act on their vision and seize opportunity. They are the ones who become entrepreneurs living into their dreams, and not someone else's!"* [page 12, *The NLE*]

In other words, it is not about looking towards what someone else is doing, per the old saying: "The grass is greener on the other side." For that is looking outside of ourselves.

Instead, Mr. A encourages us to look within ourselves: to our deepest dreams and desires. In his letter "Trekking into the Unexplored", Mr. A reveals that he has known hard battles by pursuing what is most true about himself; however, he *"cannot imagine a richer and more fulfilling life"*. [page 89, *The NLE*]

Later in the same letter, Mr. A writes: *"Max, in your letter of November 6th you will find embedded in your description of your true self, both identity and mission. Whether complete or incomplete I do not know, but your true self descriptors are connected to your deepest desires. The truest things about you are your best guide to your best future."* [page 90, *The NLE*]

Whether this Navigator is for your company or your business idea or just for you, it begins, first and foremost with you.

Remember: *"Any one with a vision for anything is an entrepreneur."* And, that's where we will start, but first let me orient you... What's that?

Can this process really be done well, in just One Hour?

Absolutely! You can produce an excellent Navigator in One Hour, assuming you have read the book, established your High Camp (more on that in a minute), and obey your timing device.

And, follow my instructions to the letter.

Be confident! You are not the first person I have guided!

So, welcome to The [One Hour] Next Level Navigator!
It's your destiny that is at stake, so remember my rhyme:

The [One Hour] Next Level Navigator is yours to achieve;
should you fail, a mediocre life is yours to receive.
Complete this challenge and you will see,
the truer person you are intended to be.

How to best use this little book

First

Read this book, including all the prompts. That's right, you will do much better, if you know what is coming next. It is estimated to be about a 30 to 45 minute read.

Second

Read *The NLE* [*Next Level Entrepreneur*] in full.

If you haven't yet finished *The NLE*, but are eager to do *The [One Hour] Next Level Navigator*, then read all of the pages in *The NLE* that are referenced in this book. This will deepen your understanding about the process and lead to better results.

The references are easy to spot, as they all say "[Sourced from *The NLE*, pages...]", and are found on pages 5, 9 (2 refs), 12, 16, 20, 22, 24, 28, and 30 (2 refs) of this book.

Third

Establish a High Camp. This is not a metaphor, it needs to be a real place for you to go. Follow all the guide's instructions. This includes creating both an envisioning list and a dream list prior to beginning the process.

Fourth

Start your timer for the [One Hour] process! It all begins at the bottom of page 11. Answer each prompt, and move on to the next one when your time expires, whether you are finished or not.

Most Important

Trust and follow the instructions of your guide in every detail! He will not steer you wrong. In so doing, you will find that your results will be much better than if you change any of his guidance.

The [One Hour]

The Map

In your hand, you will find a map.

This map is from Mr. A's document enclosed with his letter of Wednesday, January 2, 1946 called: "The essence of The Next Level Navigator" [pages 120-127, *The NLE*].

Below is his description of the map which he humorously refers to as another one of his "beautiful illustrations":

"My experience suggests a company's initial envisioning of their future may convey the basic idea, but it is a more of a placeholder. It takes time and movement towards Next Levels for envisioning to become clearer. Ultimately, a true vision is huge and will take years to accomplish, maybe more than a lifetime. That is why that vision is on the distant horizon.

I have enclosed another of my 'beautiful illustrations'. [above]

The Next Level is much closer than the horizon. It is comparable to being over a hill. The path to achieving it can not be known, yet you can know what it is. Reaching The Next

Level is always moving a company towards its vision. Time-wise, The Next Level is 3 to 5 years away.

So, what do we call what we can see to achieve? The Next Strategic Step, because the route to it can be known and usually requires 6 to 12 months. As one Next Step is achieved, the next one emerges until eventually The Next Level is reached." [pages 123-124, *The NLE*]

I would recommend before you go any further, to reread Mr. A's entire "essence" document to help orient you to The Next Level Navigator process [Sourced from *The NLE*, pages 120-127].

Tips for applying The Navigator to various circumstances

Tip #1 for a Personal Navigator: If you are seeking a personal Next Level for your life, the best results will source from knowing your deepest desires and truest things about you. If you need help with this, I suggest that you do The Sage Advice to Apply in Part One of *The NLE*.

Tip #2 for Personal Envisioning: Mr. A wrote the letter, "Dreams to Envisioning" [pages 128-129, *The NLE*] from the standpoint of a company. However, this works equally well for a person. Simply envision what your life could be like in all its facets. Imagine looking back over it 20 to 50 years from now.

Tip #3 for Undecided on a specific Business Endeavor: You will want to start by first translating your passions into what makes sense for a business. The Sage Advice to Apply in Parts 1 and 2 of *The NLE* can help sort that out. Then do *The [One Hour] Next Level Navigator* for the First Level of that endeavor.

Tip #4 for Ongoing Companies with key leaders: As the entrepreneur/owner/leader of an ongoing company, consider involving your key team leaders in this process after you have done it, first. Also, you may find doing a personal Next Level very helpful in ascertaining how your business may or may not be moving you in the direction you really want to go in life.

Tip #5 for a Career Next Level: Basically, blend Tips #1, 2, and 3. A career is similar to a business startup, but personal at the same time. In this dynamic your envisioning needs to be focused on your work life. Imagine looking back on your career and write characteristics of what would be fulfilling.

Establish a High Camp

If you were to climb The Grand Teton mountain peak in Wyoming's Teton National Park, you would establish a base camp, known as a High Camp, at 11,200 feet. It's where climbers acclimatize and make final preparations a few thousand feet below the summit. They have already hiked at least a day to reach it.

The final climb to the peak always begins in the early morning from High Camp, because by midday all kinds of weather conditions can occur in the mountains preventing a successful assault of the summit.

With a similar mindset, we need to set up a High Camp to properly prepare for your assault of *The [One Hour] Next Level Navigator.* By reading *The NLE [Next Level Entrepreneur]*, you've already hiked quite a while just to get here.

I can see you're anxious to start, but you will be astonished at how fast this hour will vanish once you begin. You will need all you wits, energy and creativity to succeed. And remember, there is no turning back, if you fail to finish in One Hour you will lose a life!

So, let's establish your High Camp, get ready, and acclimatize. You can begin your assault tomorrow morning, or the morning after, whenever you are ready.

One distraction and Your Mission is Scrubbed!

Just like weather in the mountains, any kind of interruption or distraction can pop up the further into the day you go. If you can not give this assault 110% of who you are, your creativity and your mind; then don't begin. Wait until you can completely focus and shut out everything else.

Your High Camp needs to be free from all distractions and

clutter. Isolate it from everyone and everything. Warn anyone who may need you for anything about your unavailability due to your morning assault. Until you complete The Navigator you are completely 'off the grid' that day.

That means no electronics, no people, no news or information. Do whatever it takes to make this happen.

For this One Hour you will be in the wild with only your imagination, a pen, and the paper in this book! **I repeat: there are no computers or any other electronic devices allowed on this daring assault.**

Even allowing the tiniest interruption, and the mission is scrubbed until the next morning! Ok?!?

High Camp Essentials

- Have a favorite pen with which to write. In fact, I suggest having a backup in case of failure.
- Have a timer with an alarm. Each section is timed and you need an alarm to sound, so you don't lose track of time.
  - A watch is best.
  - However, if you must use a phone as a timer, turn it to airplane mode so you can't receive any messages or calls.
  - Be ruthless with your timer. The time limit will force great ideas out of you. Afterwards, you will be surprised at how good your ideas are.
- Stay hydrated! Have plenty of water ready and quickly available throughout your One Hour assault. I am not kidding!
- Get plenty of rest the night prior to the morning of your assault. Wind down early the evening before, don't be 'cramming' on this process or worrying about anything else. The best assaults are at the beginning of your day.
- Have a good breakfast. You'll need lots of energy for this One Hour! Trust me.

Acclimate before your Morning Assault.

Once you have established your High Camp a day or two before your assault, begin acclimating to it by reading "Dreams to Envisioning" [Sourced from *The NLE*, pages 128-129]. Follow the instructions in the letter and begin listing all that you envision on a blank sheet of paper.

If you want to go a bit further, then I suggest you reread "Ready, Fire, Aim" and follow Mr. A's instructions on page 125 under the heading: "How to begin The Navigator process" [Sourced from *The NLE*, pages 117-119, 125]. On a separate blank piece of paper list your dreams.

The idea behind these readings and lists is to begin stimulating your imagination and unleashing what is most true about you, as ways to build your creative momentum for the assault.

And yes, bring these lists with you when you begin in the morning. It will give you a running start. You may even pick up some time early on, that you can apply later in the hour. Remember your assault is a sprint!

Lastly, by following these guidelines and establishing a High Camp a day or two before your morning assault, you will have appropriated every advantage for a creating and completing a great *[One Hour] Next Level Navigator*.

Right, then! Off you go.
Get that High Camp established.
And, orient yourself for your morning assault.

It's your destiny that is at stake, so remember my rhyme:

The [One Hour] Next Level Navigator is yours to achieve;
should you fail, a mediocre life is yours to receive.
Complete this challenge and you will see,
the truer person you are intended to be.

The [One Hour] process starts here, so... Let's Begin your Assault

Good morning, brave reader! The day has arrived!

Welcome to *The [One Hour] Next Level Navigator*.

You look well rested and full of energy! Within an hour you can be well on your way to your Next Level.

Your final instructions:

Each prompt has a <u>maximum time limit</u>. Set and start your timer for this time limit. Begin reading, then doing the prompt.

When the timer goes off, you must STOP!

Move to the next prompt, no matter what you are doing and restart your timer.

You will be absolutely amazed at how much you can create in these highly focused, super concentrated bursts!

If you finish before the time expires, immediately move to the next prompt. This will give you a little time cushion for later on.

There is a running total of time elapsed at the end of each prompt, so you can know exactly where you are in the One Hour.

Finally, there are extra blank pages in the back of the book if you need more writing space for any prompt.

I am sure you are ready to begin your assault.

I wish you the Best of Success! And remember...

Your destiny is in your hands!

Write the exact time you are beginning: _____.

Add 60 minutes to it and write that time on page 26.

Begin NOW!

The [One Hour]

Dreams to Envisioning

[Sourced from *The NLE*, pages 128-129, 132-135, 138]

For this undertaking you have **10 minutes.** Start your timer! Straight off you go:

We begin with your dreams that will lead you to envisioning for yourself or your business endeavor 20 to 50 years from now per Mr. A's instructions. [*The NLE*, pages 128-129 and 134-135]

Using your lists from High Camp rewrite the best and most descriptive elements from your envisioning list and dreams list (if you did one) into a single envisioning list on these 2 pages.

Be inspired to add more elements that occur to you in creating this final, blended envisioning list. The idea is to brainstorm as many elements as you can envision until your timer goes off.

Your blended envisioning list:

Blended envisioning list continued...

Total Time elapsed: <u>10 minutes</u>

The [One Hour]

As you remain in your full creativity! You have **7 minutes**. Start your timer! Move quickly to complete the following:

In **1 minute** circle your top 3 to 5 most vivid and essential elements from your blended envisioning list on pages 12-13.

In the remaining **6 minutes** combine your circled ideas into one sentence. Do not worry if it's wordy or rambling, just write it all into a single sentence. Consider this the first draft of your Envision Sentence. [Example sentence page 138, *The NLE*]

Now keep rewriting the sentence by refining, combining and shortening it. Write as many drafts as you can until the timer sounds. Don't forget that this is 20 to 50 years from now.

Your Envision Sentence drafts:

Next Level Navigator

Continuation of Envision Sentence drafts...

Now start your timer for **1 minute!**

Restate (not copy) **your final Envision Sentence.**

Total Time elapsed: 18 minutes

The [One Hour]

Your Next Level

[Sourced from *The NLE*, pages 153-157, 160-162]

Stay hydrated, you have **8 minutes.** Check the map to orient yourself to your Next Level (page 4 in this book). Start your timer!

As you consider your final Envision Sentence on page 15, what could that Next Level be for you? Remember, that per the map it moves you towards your vision, i.e. that distant horizon. Begin listing descriptive phrases and characteristics of what that Next Level could be.

Another angle to help you create more ideas for your Next Level: write the date you could reach that Next Level: _____

(minimum 3 years from now).

Imagine it is the date above and you have achieved your Next Level. Looking back over these years, what characterizes the Next Level you are now at? What has moved you from where you were to where you are 'today'? Remember, do NOT write any financial or numerical characteristics.

Your Next Level characteristics:

Next Level Navigator

Next Level characteristics continued...

Total Time elapsed: <u>26 minutes</u>

The [One Hour]

You're looking great! Keep up the pace! For this prompt you have **4 minutes.** Start your timer!

How do you know when you've reached your Next Level? In other words, what marks the finish line? You need to know, so you can have a great celebration!

Look over all the Next Level characteristics you wrote on the previous 2 pages. Now imagine completing every single one of them. What would indicate you have completed them? What would mark that you had actually achieved each characteristic?

List all the Next Level finish line markers: (you can think of)

Next Level Navigator

Continuing your Next Level markers list...

For this step you have **1 minute.** Start your timer!

Circle the top 3 to 5 most important markers.

[You may select only 1 financial and/or 1 numerical metric.]

These are the 3 - 5 Key Markers that delineate your Next Level finish line.

Total Time elapsed: 31 minutes

The [One Hour]

Time to catch your 2nd wind. Dig deep on this one!

Craft your Next Level sentence in the next 7 minutes.

Start your timer!

[Sourced from *The NLE*, page 205]

Review all your Next Level characteristics (pages 16-17) and in **1 minute** circle the 3 to 5 best ones that describe your Next Level.

Remember! Your Next Level is 3 to 5 years from now, and moves you towards your vision, and you 'can know what it is, but not know how to get there.' So, do NOT select any characteristics that you can see a path on how you would accomplish it.

In the remaining **6 minutes** blend your top 3 to 5 characteristics into a single sentence. Similar to writing the Envision Sentence, do not worry about its wordiness or clumsy expression. Simply get all of it down on paper as a single sentence. Continue to restate and refine the thoughts contained in the sentence by rewriting as many drafts as there is time for.

Drafts of your Next Level sentence:

Next Level Navigator

Continuation of Next Level sentence drafts:

Now start your timer for **1 minute!**

Restate (not copy) **your final Next Level sentence.**

Total Time elapsed: <u>39 minutes</u>

The [One Hour]

Success Barriers

[Sourced from *The NLE*, pages 163-165, 168-169]

I don't want you to get all negative, like Max. So, you only have **4 minutes**. Start your timer! And, run this gauntlet fast!

Keep rereading your Next Level sentence on page 21, and answer this question: What are the first things that come to mind that you must overcome to begin moving towards your Next Level?

These are Success Barriers! So, list the most immediate and most formidable Success Barriers you can think of that could prevent you from beginning to move towards your Next Level.

Write those Success Barriers in 3 minutes:

Continue listing your Success Barriers:

1 minute before the timer goes off:

Circle and rewrite the SINGLE largest, most immediate, and formidable Success Barrier.

Hint: You may have listed several immediate barriers. If it makes sense, then combine them into 1 barrier.

This is THE SINGLE SUCCESS BARRIER that could keep you from making headway towards your Next Level.

Total Time elapsed: <u>43 minutes</u>

The [One Hour]

Next Strategic Steps

[Sourced from *The NLE*, pages 173-186]

You're almost to the summit! Push hard, be super positive, and use every ounce of creativity you have left! You have **7 minutes.** Start your timer! Now go, you're almost there!

Keep an eye on your single, immediate Success Barrier on page 23. Brainstorm every strategy you can think of to overcome it.

Don't pause and analyze your strategies, just sling them on to these 2 pages. Let them come up from your gut. These strategies are ways to breakthrough this single Success Barrier, so can you make headway towards your Next Level.

Use 6 minutes to create strategies:

More of your strategies...

1 minute before the timer goes off:

Circle the absolute best 3 to 5 strategies that will bust through your single, most immediate, and formidable Success Barrier.

These are your Next Strategic Steps!

Total Time elapsed: 50 minutes

The [One Hour] Next Level Navigator instructions (page 26) *& final form* (page 27)

[*With pages 26 and 27 next to each other,* **write your answers on page 27.**]

Congratulations! You are about **10 minutes** away from "The Summit". Now, it's time to complete the final form.

Write 60 minutes from you start time here:_____

Write the time you arrived at this page here:_____

Write the difference in the 2 times here:_____

Start your timer for the difference.

1. Turn to page 15, restate your Envision Sentence, down there.

2. Turn to pages 16-17, restate your top 3 to 5 Next Level characteristics, over here.

3. Turn to page 18-19, restate your top 3 to 5 Key Markers, up here.

4. Turn to page 21, and restate your Next Level sentence, up here.

6. This section is optional. Turn to page 28 for instructions. Although, this section is helpful towards your Next Level, it is not part of the One Hour.

5. Turn to page 24-25, restate your best 3 to 5 Next Strategic Steps in the order that you would pursue them, here.

7. See the breakthrough arrow on page 27: In the box above it summarize the Next Level in 3 words. In the circle below it summarize the strengths in 3 words.

Form header:

- Under 'begin' write today's date.
- Next to 'for' write your name or company's.
- Under 'complete' write the date on page 16.

Total Time elapsed: [One Hour]!

begin   The Next Level Navigator™ for_____   complete
_/_/__   _/_/__

Next level sentence: (3 to 5 years)

Key Markers:

Characteristics:

-
-
-
-
-

Success Barriers to break through

Next Strategic Steps: (in 1 year)

1.
2.
3.
4.
5.

Strengths to build on:

Envision Sentence:

List Current Level characteristics to build on for Next Level, such as: Guiding Principles, Current Strengths, etc.:

-
-
-
-
-

Copyright © 2018 by George Black, Published by Intigro Press, LLC and in association with Intigro, Inc. from the book: *The [One Hour] Next Level Navigator*. Used with permission for the sole and express use of readers of this book. Available at Amazon.com.

The [One Hour]

One Hour +, if you have 5 minutes

[(Example is) Sourced from *The NLE*, page 151]

While you are up top here on The Summit, if you have **5 minutes** take a crack at this last prompt! Start your timer!

The idea of this section in The Navigator is to identify and list your current (level) strengths within yourself or your company that will propel you to the Next Level. Essentially, these are the very best attributes of your current level that you want to keep.

I did not include this in the *[One Hour]* for the sake of time. So, without going through all the processes of a complete Navigator, simply brainstorm a list of strengths, which can certainly include Guiding Principles, etc.

Use 4 minutes to brainstorm your list of strengths:

Continuation of strengths list:

Now use your final **1 minute** to **circle your most robust 3 to 6 strengths.** Then, **rewrite them** onto the bottom section of your Navigator form on page 27.

Total Time elapsed: <u>65 minutes</u>

A Closing Word from George

Well done, fearless reader and gamer! You have charted your destiny, now the real adventure begins!

And this is no game; it's real life. But do not worry, remember the words of Mr. A: *"... life becomes a real adventure for those who act on their vision and seize opportunity."*

You have reached The Summit and completed *The [One Hour] Next Level Navigator!* Congratulations, few achieve such clarity and strategy.

Pause. Look around. Enjoy your accomplishment! For you see, in reality you stand on that precipice overlooking the valley of your future that Max describes in his letter "A Precipice" [Sourced from *The NLE*, pages 32-34]. Later, Mr. A will encourage Max to return to that precipice in his letter "More to Know" [Sourced from *The NLE*, pages 103-104].

> **Now, it's time to step off into your Next Strategic Steps!**
> Keep your Navigator close at hand and visible! *Read it daily!* Display it on your desk or wall. It must always be top of mind!

For I have every confidence that you have what it takes to negotiate the opportunities and challenges that lie ahead.

Unfortunately, I must bid you adieu. But there is no reason we can not meet again to plan the navigation of the next leg of your adventure.

In the meantime, stay in touch and let us know of your progress. Drop a line any time to IdeasFor@livetrulyfree.com.

I wish you the very best of success and to *Live Truly Free!*

~ George Black
July, 2018

More resources to reach your Next Level!

As Max writes to Mr. A:
> *"...I would prefer to chart my own course,
> rather than work as a part of another person's vision."*

To that end, we've launched:

Live Truly Free

www.LiveTrulyFree.com

To help every entrepreneur at any level
"chart their own course"
by providing practical business guidance and strategy.
You're not alone in your **Entrepreneurial Trek**.
We're here to come alongside you!
So...
What are you needing as an entrepreneur?
Please tell us at
www.LiveTrulyFree.com/trek

And let's make

Live Truly Free

your 'go to' site for entrepreneurial help!

Plus...
**We would love to give you a FREE copy of
The Next Level Navigator form!**
(like the one on page 196.)
www.LiveTrulyFree.com/trek

About the Author

George Black guides entrepreneurs / business owners to develop their best strategies, create sustainable profits and build a great company.

He is both an entrepreneur and author.

Plus, George loves entrepreneurs!

He wants every entrepreneur to reap the same benefits as his 1 on 1 clients. So, George shares the same proven processes in *The Next Level Entrepreneur* that he has used to help numerous entrepreneurs, business owners, and companies for years.

Now, he and his team have launched Live Truly Free at LiveTrulyFree.com to begin providing even more resources for any entrepreneur who wants to build a great company.

Since 1992, George has worked as a Business Strategist and Outsourced Chief Financial Officer (CFO) through his company Intigro, www.intigro.com, where he created The Next Level Navigator®.

His clients have experienced significant growth, great breakthroughs, and increased profits.

Most notably, he applied his expertise and The Next Level Navigator at Rackspace Hosting for 4 years. He helped guide their corporate strategy as revenues grew five times to $500m and their going public (NYSE: RAX).

George has worked with businesses of all sizes across the U.S. and abroad in technology, software as a service, manufacturing, commercial sales, professional firms, engineering, construction, government contracting, and not for profits.

George resides in San Antonio, Texas and has 2 sons. Some of his other passions include backpacking, travel, healthy living and helping 'the least of these'.

Your Personal Notes & Insights

These final pages are for you brave reader and gamer! Write to your heart's content all the ideas and insights you may have gotten in this process that are not captured on the previous pages.

And be aware that even more ideas will continue bubbling up from your vast creative stores that have been stirred, even after completing The Navigator.

Write them on these pages, so you don't lose them!

Your Personal Notes & Insights

Your Personal Notes & Insights

Your Personal Notes & Insights

Your Personal Notes & Insights

www.ingramcontent.com/pod-product-compliance
Lightning Source LLC
Chambersburg PA
CBHW080010050426
42446CB00036B/3361